BATTING CHAMPS

Jonathan Bliss

The Rourke Corporation, Inc.
Vero Beach, Florida 92964

The Rourke Corporation, Inc.
P.O. Box 3328, Vero Beach, FL 32964

Bliss, Jonathan.
    Batting champs / by Jonathan Bliss.
        p. cm. — (Baseball heroes)
    Includes bibliographical references (p. 47) and index.
    ISBN 0-86593-129-1
        1. Baseball players—United States—Biography—Juvenile literature.   2. Batting
(Baseball)—Juvenile literature.   I Title.   II. Series.
GV865.A1B58   1991
796.357'092'2—dc20   91-10205
                                                                                              CIP
                                                                                               AC

Series Editor: Gregory Lee
Editor: Marguerite Aronowitz
Book design and production: The Creative Spark, Capistrano Beach, CA
Cover photograph: Vleisides Photo/Kansas City Royals
Consultant: Rick Albrecht

Contents

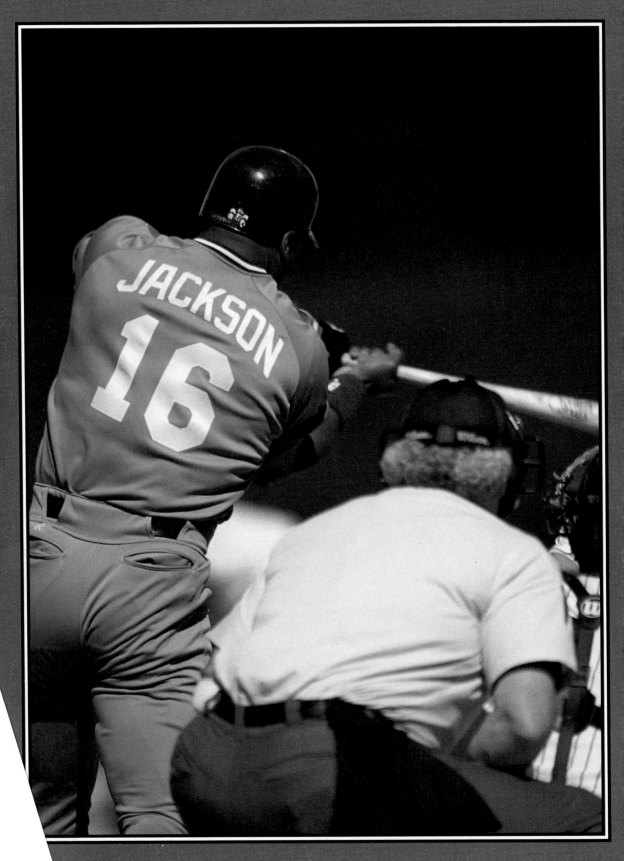

The hitter's number one job: making contact.

How Do They Do It?

There is nothing in sports so difficult as hitting a baseball. Scientists who study such things think it should be impossible to hit a ball the size of your fist when it is hurled at speeds of up to 100 miles per hour. The batter has less than one-tenth of a second to calculate the direction, location and speed of the ball, bring his hands forward, and hit the ball as it streaks past him. And he does it with a piece of wood that is no more than two and three-quarter inches in diameter. Hitting a baseball practically defies the laws of physics.

To make it harder, the pitcher has the advantage of elevation, throwing from a mound about one foot above the rest of the playing surface. He has the element of surprise, for he can throw the ball so that it curves, dips, or rises as it reaches home plate.

And that's not all! The hitter must make solid contact between a bat with a curved surface

Eddie Murray fouls off a tough pitch.

7

Making contact isn't enough.
Now Vince Coleman must hustle to first base.

l a round ball. Even to nick the ball with your bat
ald be difficult. To hit it solidly seems impossible. It
ld be bad enough if the bat were flat and the ball
twice as large.

Just hitting the ball should be enough, but it isn't.
ales of baseball say you must hit the ball well
h to get you to first base before the ball gets there.
eans you must hit the ball over or through the
fenders on the field. With all these obstacles, the
baseball seems entirely too difficult for anyone
, let alone play it well.

plenty of talented people do.

Great Hitters Are Rare

Baseball became popular in the late 1800s. In those early days, it was difficult for a batter to hit the baseball with any real consistency. Most versions of the game required that the pitcher throw the ball slowly enough for the hitter to be able to make contact. Even so, a winning team depended more on its fielding than on its hitting.

Thousands of athletes have played baseball professionally since the 1860s, yet because of the difficulty of the sport, there have been few great hitters. An average batter is typically a player who can get a hit once every five times at bat. That's a batting average above .200. A capable hitter is anyone who manages to get a hit once every four times at bat, or .250. There are players in the National Baseball Hall of Fame in Cooperstown, New York, who have lifetime batting averages around .250. That means that even though they were called out three of every four times at bat, they were still considered good, or even great hitters.

Any batter who manages to break the .300 average, even for a single season, assures himself of being among the five or ten best hitters in his league. So rare is it for a player to get a hit once every three times at bat (.333) that very few manage to do it in a decade. Just one season of .300 hitting makes a player a star. During the entire history of baseball, fewer than 100 men have ever had a season with an average of .333 or higher.

What then should we think of the players who have averaged .333 in their careers? These are the true batting champs: a select group of athletes, almost all of whom are now in the Hall of Fame.

In The Beginning

The history of the great hitters began 100 years ago. Before that, the game was more like slow-pitch softball. Pitchers tossed the ball so that the hitter would have a fair chance of getting a hit. In fact, since there were no called balls or strikes, a batter could stand at home plate all day waiting for a pitch he could hit. In fact, the main emphasis of baseball scoring wasn't on hitting the ball, but on running the bases. The great stars of the early game were usually fast enough to get to first base without much trouble. Averages of .300 and over were common.

Any hit was called fair as long as it landed inside the baselines, whether it rolled out or not before reaching first base. This was called the fair-foul hit.

This rule and others made it difficult to judge the greatness of a hitter, especially by today's standards. The hitter had most of the advantages, and the emphasis was on scoring large numbers of runs. It was common to have games in which each team scored 20 or) runs.

But by 1887 baseball was changing fast. First ne called strikes and balls, then the adoption of ling mitts to help players catch more easily. This put nd to the "fair-foul" hit. In addition, pitchers were allowed to throw overhand. This led to the arance of the screwball, the fastball, the curveball, veral other kinds of pitches that were never strictly like the spitball. To help balance things out a bit, cher's mound was put back ten feet to its present 1: sixty and one-half feet from home plate.

1e result was predictable. The number of .300 ell into the single digits. Even though a walk counted as a "hit" until 1898 (the official r of the modern era), it did not help most the league.

)

Willy Keeler

One hitting star of this early era was "Wee Willie" Keeler. He was a short, brainy player who perfected a swing that drove major league pitchers crazy for more than a decade. Keeler's secret was simple: he used a big bat and choked way up on it for maximum control.

Keeler directed the ball toward the "holes" in the infield. As he put it himself: "Keep your eye on the ball and hit 'em where they ain't." Keeler was also one of the greatest all-time bunters, and along with John McGraw is credited with having perfected the hit-and-run play.

The result of his batting mastery was an outstanding career. Over a six-year period from 1894 to 1899, Keeler averaged 148 runs, 47 stolen bases, and 219 hits per year. These numbers provided him with one of the flashiest batting averages of any era: .388.

But Keeler's greatest year was 1897 when he did everything right. That year, he hit safely in 44 games—a record that stood for 44 years until Joe DiMaggio's 56-game hitting streak in 1941. Keeler ended the year with a .432 batting average, third highest all-time behind Hugh Duffy and Tip O'Neill. In 1939, Keeler was among the first two dozen players elected to the Baseball Hall of Fame.

...meiro had an outstanding season in 1990, hitting .319
in a run at the AL batting title.

The Modern Era

Although many great hitters had played in the 19th century, their rules were considerably different from those of today. But by 1903, baseball had taken on its present form, and the major leagues crawled with pitchers who could make any batter tremble like Cy Young, Walter "Big Train" Johnson, and Christy Mathewson. Infielders were quicker, outfielders more mobile, and the umpires more likely to call strikes.

One of the era's greatest hitters was Honus Wagner. Called "The Flying Dutchman" by his teammates, Wagner made pitcher's lives

Kirby Puckett had baseball's third-highest batting average in the 1980s.

Honus Wagner never batted less than .300 in his entire career.

miserable for 25 years, as he led Pittsburgh to NL
pennants four times and helped them win the World
Series in 1909. During these years, Wagner won the
batting title eight times and paced the National League
in RBIs four times.

With a .329 career batting average and a .469
slugging average (eighth all-time), Wagner compiled
1,740 runs, 3,430 hits, 651 doubles, 252 triples, 101
home runs, 1,732 RBIs, and 722 stolen bases! In 1917,
at the age of 43, he finally retired, having never batted
below .300 in any season.

Tris Speaker
Tris Speaker is an example of how important

determination can be. Unlike Honus Wagner, Speaker took time to mature in the majors. In fact, his first try in the big leagues resulted in a mediocre performance.

With the Red Sox from 1909 to 1915, Speaker finally became an American League (AL) star and helped the Red Sox capture the world championship in 1912 and 1915. In 1916 he was traded to Cleveland, after the Red Sox tried to cut his $11,000 annual salary by $2,000.

Speaker would make Boston regret that $2,000. With Cleveland for eleven seasons, Speaker batted .354. A major leaguer for 22 years, Tris Speaker ranks sixth overall in career batting average: .344. During his entire batting career, he struck out only 220 times.

Rogers Hornsby

Surely one of the greatest hitters ever to play the game was Rogers Hornsby. An aggressive player with a fierce will, Hornsby played infield—usually second base—for the Cardinals from 1916 through 1926. From 1920 through 1925, Hornsby won six consecutive batting titles (an NL record). In those six years he batted over .400 three times, including the modern season record for highest average (.424) in 1924. At the same time, he led the NL in home runs (twice), RBIs (three times), and base hits (four times).

"Shoeless" Joe Jackson

Imagine batting over .400 in your rookie season! That's what "Shoeless" Joe Jackson did. From 1910 to 1915, he compiled batting averages ranging from .331 to .408 for the Cleveland Indians. In 1911 he batted .408, and for the next eight years Ty Cobb and Jackson fought each other for the league batting championship. But while Cobb produced singles, Jackson hit with power to all fields.

Over his 1,330 games, Jackson made 1,774 hits,

Veteran Robin Yount has had six .300 or higher seasons in his career.

knocked in 785 runs, and stole 202 bases for a career batting average of .356, third only to Cobb and Hornsby.

In 1919, eight Chicago players—including Jackson—were accused of taking bribes from gamblers in exchange for throwing the World Series. The truth was that Jackson had reluctantly taken $5,000, but he made no attempt to throw the Series. He even batted .375. Despite the fact that Jackson was found not guilty, Baseball Commissioner Kenesaw Mountain Landis barred Jackson from organized baseball for life. Because of Jackson's expulsion from baseball, he was never elected into the Hall of Fame.

Ty Cobb

The greatest hitter of his era—many people would say the greatest hitter of any era—was Ty Cobb. His father wanted him to go to school, but Cobb preferred baseball. In 1904, at the age of 17, he became a professional ballplayer. By 1905 his performance caught the eye of the Detroit Tigers. By the time he retired 24 years later, Ty Cobb held 43 major league regular season and career records. As a measure of Cobb's greatness, many of those records have never been broken, and others stood for many decades.

Cobb played "scientific" baseball, featuring aggressive base running and batting to counter the great pitching of the era. No one ever ran the bases with more daring than Cobb, who perfected the hook slide. Cobb was taller than most of the other great stealers, but what he gave up in speed he made up for in rough play. For example, to discourage infielders from tagging him out, he would sharpen his cleats and slide into base with his feet up.

At the plate he held the bat with his hands apart and stood well back in the batter's box to give himself time to react to the pitch. And Cobb practiced tirelessly. Between 1907 and 1915, Cobb won nine AL batting titles in a row and added three more between 1917 and 1919. He hit at least .320 for 23 straight years, capped by brilliant seasons of .401, .410, and .420. His best season was in 1911, when he led the AL in every offensive category except home runs.

How great was Cobb? He led the AL in batting average 12 times, slugging percentage eight times, hits seven times, stolen bases six times, and runs five times.

No one was more feared at the plate or on the base paths than the legendary Ty Cobb.

He had at least 200 hits for nine seasons and stole a career-high 96 bases in 1915.

Cobb was not well liked by his fellow ballplayers. They considered him to be overly aggressive and difficult to get along with. Despite this, Cobb was well-liked by the fans, and he remains one of the two or three greatest players ever to step on a baseball diamond.

Lou Gehrig

Pity the poor pitcher. If Babe Ruth weren't bad enough, opposing pitchers had to face Lou Gehrig on the same team. After two seasons in the minors, Gehrig

"The Iron Horse"—Lou Gehrig. The left-hander played for many seasons with Babe Ruth, forming the most awesome power duo in baseball history.

became a regular player for the Yankees in 1925 and never left the lineup. He established the all-time record for the most consecutive games played—an incredible 2,130 games. No wonder that his teammates and the fans called him "The Iron Horse."

Gehrig and Ruth were always competing for the best batting stats. In 1927, for example, when Ruth slugged 60 homers, Gehrig slapped 47. In most other categories, the left-handed Gehrig surpassed Ruth,

Babe Ruth was a great hitter for both average and power.
He was also the highest paid player during the Great Depression.

batting .373 and leading the AL in doubles and total bases. Gehrig also broke the record for most major league RBIs in one season, 175.

Gehrig continued playing flawless baseball, scoring and knocking in over 100 runs for 13 straight seasons. He won the Triple Crown of hitting (home runs, batting average, and RBIs) in 1927, 1934, and 1937. He became the first AL player ever to hit four home runs in one game on June 3, 1932. Gehrig also had 23 grand slam homers. Quiet and modest, Gehrig was nonetheless a fierce competitor on the field, piling up some of the most impressive career statistics ever earned: 535 doubles, 493 home runs, 1,188 runs scored, and 1,990 RBIs.

In 1939 at the age of 35, the Iron Horse developed a rare muscle disease (afterwards known as Lou Gehrig's Disease) which forced his early retirement and claimed his life a few years later.

Babe Ruth

No figure in American athletic history was more written about or idolized than George Herman "Babe" Ruth. The son of a saloon keeper, Ruth was put in an orphanage when he was seven where he learned both a trade and baseball. By 1914, Ruth's remarkable ability as a left-handed pitcher prompted the Baltimore Orioles to sign him. He was traded to the Boston Red Sox in 1915, and won world championships for them the next two years. He set a record for scoreless innings pitched in World Series play.

Even though he was probably the best pitcher in the major leagues at the time, he proved to be an even better hitter. His incredible batting talent persuaded his manager to put him in the outfield. In 1919, the left-hander set a major league record with 29 home runs.

Boston fans were outraged when the Red Sox traded Ruth to the New York Yankees in 1920. From 1920 to his release in 1934, Ruth ruled the major leagues, putting up incredible numbers every year. Although he is remembered today as a home run hitter (714 lifetime), Ruth was also a great hitter for average. He was routinely either at the top or near the top of the batting lead, and compiled a lifetime batting average of .342. This combination of power and hitting has never been equaled by any other ballplayer. Even more impressive, the Yankees superstar led his team to seven AL pennants and four World Series titles.

In 1936 Ruth was elected a charter member of the Hall of Fame. Even today, Babe Ruth is recognized as the finest all-around player ever to play the game.

Kevin Mitchell's performance in 1989 earned him NL MVP honors.

The National Pastime

The period from 1940 through 1970 was a golden age for baseball. It seemed that everything having to do with the sport got bigger. The leagues expanded and the stadiums and crowds grew larger. Salaries rose, the size of the athletes increased—even the baseball mitt got larger. Aided by radio and later by television, baseball became the true national pastime. Some of the announcers, like Mel Allen and Vin Scully, became as famous as the players they described.

It was also the era of the great Yankee teams. Talented players such as Joe DiMaggio, Mickey Mantle and Roger Maris made the Yanks virtually unstoppable. They won the AL pennant an amazing 17 times in 30 years, and 12 world championships.

Joe DiMaggio

Joe DiMaggio carried on the tradition of great New York Yankee baseball. He entered professional baseball in 1931 at age 17. He was promoted to the big leagues and the Yankees in 1936, where he remained for 16 years. As a rookie, he hit .323 and slugged 29 home runs. He tied for the AL lead in triples and paced the AL's outfields in assists. From there he only got better. Despite the large confines of Yankee Stadium, DiMaggio always hit well there. And he hit even better on the road, averaging one homer every 16 times at bat.

DiMaggio served three years in the military in the middle of his career. It had no effect on his greatness. He has a career batting average of .325. He was named

Mickey Mantle, just another member of an exclusive club: Yankee batting champs.

the league's Most Valuable Player (MVP) in 1939-41, with 361 total home runs. But perhaps the record "The Yankee Clipper" is best known for was set in 1941, just before he enlisted and went off to war. In that incredible season, DiMaggio got at least one hit in 56 straight games, a record that has never been broken.

Mickey Mantle

When you think of the New York Yankees in the '30s, you think of Ruth and Gehrig. In the '40s it was DiMaggio, and in the '50s and '60s, it was Mickey Mantle.

At the age of seven Mantle's father trained him to be a switch-hitter. By the time he was a teenager, Mantle was signed to his first pro baseball contract— three weeks out of high school. In 1951, at age 20, the Mick was signed to a big league contract.

Playing next to Joe DiMaggio was tough for a kid from Oklahoma, and Mantle didn't do very well his first year. After that, however, Mantle led the club in home runs and batting almost every year. Despite many leg injuries, Mantle had a great 18-year career. When he retired in 1968, the Mick had hit 2,415 hits in only 2,401 games, slugged 536 homers, and earned a .298 career batting average. In 1956, Mantle won the Triple Crown with a .353 batting average, 52 homers, and 130 RBIs.

In 1961, he engaged in the greatest home run duel in baseball history with his teammate, Roger Maris. Neck and neck most of the year, Mantle went down with an injury near the end of the season and hobbled home with 54 round-trippers while Maris scored a record 61. But Mantle's worth to the Yanks cannot be judged by just statistics alone. During his time with the Yankees, the club won the World Series seven times.

Ted Williams

Ask for the sport's greatest "pure hitters," and

The man with the perfect swing: Boston's Ted Williams.

three names will always come up: Ty Cobb, Rogers Hornsby, and Ted Williams. "The Splendid Splinter" may have been the best hitter of the three, since he was not only a great hitter but a power hitter as well.

Ted hit .327 in his first season, and led the AL in RBIs. He was named Rookie of the Year (given to the best first-year player in each league). In 1941 Ted hit .402. He was the youngest player ever to break the .400 barrier, and the last player ever to do it. Twenty-eight years later, in 1958, Williams was still challenging pitchers with that same graceful, perfect swing. At age 39 he became the oldest player to win a batting title. He repeated this the following year as well, when he batted .328. With sharp eyesight and quick wrists, Williams could do anything he wanted to on the baseball diamond.

When he retired in 1960 after 19 years in Boston, Williams had career marks like these: second ever in walks (2,019) and slugging percentage (.634), and sixth all-time in batting average (.344). A left-handed batter who fielded right-handed, Williams was named to every All-Star Game for 20 years. All this even though five of his best playing years were lost to military service in two wars. His record clearly shows that he ranks second only to Babe Ruth in power and batting average.

Stan Musial

What Williams was for the American League, Stan "the Man" Musial was for the National League. Born and raised in a Pennsylvania steel mill town, Stan chose baseball over college in 1938 when he began life in the pros as a left-handed pitcher for a St. Louis Cardinals farm club. And he was good, compiling an impressive 18-5 record his first year. When Musial damaged his shoulder, he was converted to a full-time outfielder. From 1941 until 1963 he played outfield and first base for the St. Louis Cardinals.

The durable Pedro Guerrero has more than 1,400 hits in his career.

Combining speed, fielding, and hitting, Musial led the Cardinals to four NL pennants and three world championships in his first four years. Musial also won seven batting championships. In 1948, he hit a career-high .376. He also led the league several times in triples, doubles, total bases, RBIs, and slugging average. Until Hank Aaron broke them, Musial held NL career records for games played, at bats, runs scored, and RBIs.

Musial batted a career .340 through the 1958 season, but stayed in the game for another five years. He averaged only .283 over those years, bringing his career average down to .331. But this was still good enough to rank him among the best hitters to ever play the game. By the time he retired at age 43, Stan had won most of the honors baseball could give him, including three MVP awards. In 1969, his first year of eligibility, Musial was named to the Hall of Fame.

Roberto Clemente

Roberto Clemente came out of the cane fields of Puerto Rico. A poor farmer's kid, he turned into one of the finest players of his day and a legend in his island country.

Drafted by the Pirates in 1954, Clemente joined the majors in 1955 and spent the rest of his major league career in Pittsburgh. During the 1960s, the right-hander won four NL batting titles. He regularly topped the league in hits, triples, and fielding assists. During his career, he batted above .300 13 times on his way to becoming the 11th major leaguer to reach 3,000 hits. He could always be counted on for a hit when it really mattered.

Clemente was one of the first of the great Latin American ballplayers, and he helped many others reach the majors. He never forgot his roots, and became a folk hero in Puerto Rico for his many projects that helped

Jim Rice was one of the best hitters in the 1970s, winning the American League MVP award and gaining more total bases (406) in a single season than any other player since the era of Babe Ruth.

underprivileged children. In 1972, while helping to organize relief efforts after a Nicaraguan earthquake, his plane crashed shortly after takeoff and he was killed.

He left behind him a dazzling record: a .317 career batting average, 440 doubles, 166 triples, and 1,305 RBIs in just 13 seasons. In addition, he led the Pirates to two world championships: 1960 and 1971. His all-around talents earned him the NL's MVP award in 1960 and 1971, and led to his early enshrinement in the Hall of Fame, only 11 weeks after his funeral.

Willie Mays

Willie Mays always had a smile for everyone, even the pitchers he routinely beat at the plate. Brought up by his aunt in Alabama, Mays became an all-star athlete in high school. Like many future sports stars, he had his choice of at least three professional sporting careers. He chose baseball, and the rest is history.

He began his career with the New York Giants in 1951, earning Rookie of the Year. After serving in the Army, Mays returned to his team in 1954 and captured the NL batting title with an impressive .345 average. And more important, Willie led the Giants to the NL pennant and world championship. The highlight of that World Series was a spectacular catch Mays made on Vic Wertz's fly ball to deep center.

Playing with the Giants in New York and San Francisco, Mays continued to amaze the crowds, batting over .300 ten times. He led the NL in home runs four times, slugging 51 in 1955 and 52 in 1965. He also hit more than 30 home runs in 11 seasons, and scored over 100 runs 12 seasons in a row. Mays once slugged four home runs in one game and three in another game twice—a rare feat. He became the first player ever to hit at least 50 homers and steal at least 20 bases in a season (1955). He still remains one of only six players to

*Alan Trammell has joined a small club: he's one of the six
shortstops in major league history with six .300-hitting seasons.*

hit 30 home runs and steal 30 bases in the same season.

Mays retired in 1973 after a spectacular 22-year career with 3,283 hits, 660 home runs, 1,903 RBIs, a .981 fielding average, and a .302 batting average. His 660 home runs ranks third on the all-time list behind Henry Aaron and Babe Ruth. Inducted into the Hall of Fame in 1979, Willie Mays is still involved in baseball as a coach.

Rod Carew's hitting skill season after season landed him in the Hall of Fame in 1991.

Today's Greats

The modern era of baseball has featured many changes in the grand old game, such as the addition of relief pitchers. For batters, it was hard enough when pitchers only had the curve and the fastball. Today there are a whole range of pitches, including the knuckleball and slider, that have made hitting even more difficult.

The relief pitcher brings a fresh arm into the lineup whenever the starting pitcher begins to tire. Using this new technique, managers have made life very difficult for batters during the last three decades. Maybe that's why no batter has broken the .400 level since Ted Williams did it in 1941. Nonetheless, there have been a number of outstanding batting champions in the last 20 years, several of them still playing today.

Rod Carew

Rod Carew combined speed and precise hitting that made him one of the best at getting on base. Hospitalized with rheumatic fever at the age of 11, Carew worked hard to build himself up as a young man by playing baseball. In time he was hitting too well to play with his own age group.

In 1967 he joined the Minnesota Twins and batted .292 his first year, winning Rookie of the Year honors. Batting left and fielding right-handed, Carew soon became the most important member of the Twins lineup. He played both second and first base for them. In 1978, Carew was traded to the California Angels, where he

The man with the most career hits is Pete Rose, with an incredible 4,256.

played until his retirement in 1985.

During his 18 seasons in the majors, Carew hit above .300 15 times and won seven AL batting titles. He was the AL's MVP and Player of the Year in 1977, when he achieved career highs in at-bats, batting average (.388), hits (239), and other categories. Over his entire career he hit .328, and became only the 16th player to make 3,000 career hits. He was elected to the Hall of Fame in his first year of eligibility in 1990.

Pete Rose

No one ever hit the ball as well for as long as Pete Rose. Brought up in Cincinnati, Ohio, Pete had the rare opportunity to play in his home town, and he didn't waste it. Signed after high school by the Reds, the switch-hitting Rose had trouble his first few years in the minor leagues. Through practice and just plain desire, however, Rose became an aggressive hitter and fielder. Whitey Ford nicknamed him "Charley Hustle" and the name stuck, because it fit him so well. The guy was always hustling, whether on the field or off.

Although his first full year in the majors won him a Rookie of the Year honor in 1963, he wasn't pleased with his .273 average. Off-season drills and playing winter ball in Venezuela helped develop Rose into a star. In 1965, he hit over .300 for the first of 15 seasons. He shifted to outfield the next year and became outstanding at that position.

By 1970, Rose became a member of one of the most feared baseball clubs of all-time: "The Big Red Machine." The Reds had Johnny Bench, Joe Morgan, Tony Perez, and George Foster. They won the World Series in 1970, 1972, 1975, and 1976. Later, Rose played first base for the Phillies in the 1980 and 1983 World Series.

Rose always kept himself in shape. He was able to play longer and better than many other ballplayers of previous eras, which helped him achieve the records he did. He remains the only player ever to appear in over 500 games at five different positions and made the NL All-Star Team at each one. Through 24 seasons Rose piled up the numbers, the greatest being his record of 4,256 hits, passing even the great Ty Cobb. Rose racked up 200 or more hits ten times, a major league record. A lifetime .303 batter, Rose remains the only player besides Cobb with over 4,000 hits in his career.

Rose also proved to be a fine coach and manager of the Reds after his playing days ended in 1986, but the hustle that had made him such a great hitter on the field caught up with him off the field. Convicted of gambling and tax evasion, Rose was sent to prison in 1990 for six months and was banned from baseball for life.

Tony Gwynn

By 1988 Tony Gwynn had established himself as the outstanding hitter for average in the National League. San Diego's third-round choice in 1981, Gwynn quickly moved to the majors after one year in the minors. Despite a broken wrist in 1982, Gwynn demonstrated strong batting ability. He became the first Padre to reach 200 hits. In 1984 he captured the first batting title for that club with an average of .351. In 1987 through 1989, Gwynn again won batting title honors with averages of .369, .330 and .313.

Gwynn's 1987 season was the greatest offensive show in Padres history. His .369 average was the NL's finest since Stan Musial's .376 in 1948. Originally a weak fielder, Gwynn has become one of the best in the National League, winning four Gold Gloves in six years. A tough batter to strike out, Gwynn tied a record with five stolen bases in one game in 1986. To date, Gwynn has compiled a career .332 average over only nine major league seasons.

Rickey Henderson

In just over a decade, Rickey Henderson is already called the finest lead-off man in baseball history. Henderson came to the majors by way of the Oakland

The National League batting champion in three straight seasons
(1987-89) was Tony Gwynn.

A's in 1979. He quickly became the premier base stealer in the game. In 1980 he stole 100 bases in one season. In 1982 Henderson broke Lou Brock's major league record with 136 steals in one season. In 1984 Henderson was traded to the New York Yankees where he continued to hit singles, steal bases, and improve his power figures.

In 1985 Henderson became the first AL player ever with a 20-homer, 50-steal season, when he hit 24 round-trippers and stole 80 bases. He repeated this feat in 1986. He broke Bobby Bonds' career record for most lead-off home runs (35) in 1989, and has led the AL three times in runs scored. He has scored at least 100 runs in nine seasons. Henderson has been the leader of an Oakland team that went to the World Series three years in a row. During that time, he has ranked amongst the top hitters every year.

Henderson was selected the MVP for the 1989 League Championship Series, then hit .474 in the World Series when the A's defeated the Giants.

George Brett

George Brett came from a baseball family. His older brother, Ken, pitched for 13 years in the majors while two other brothers played minor league ball. George was a slow starter. He hit only .125 in his first major league call-up, and hit only two home runs with 47 RBIs his first full season with the Kansas City Royals.

But when Brett blossomed, he became one of the best hitters in baseball. Brett credits much of his success to his batting coach, Charley Lau, who trained him to lean back in the batting box, crouch slightly, and adapt to what pitchers offered instead of waiting for fastballs. He led the AL in hits and triples his second season, while batting .308. He won his first batting title in 1976 when he batted .333, beating out teammate Hal

Rickey Henderson's hitting power has helped him become the top base stealer of the '90s.

Pirates outfield sensation Barry Bonds joins a major league club of great RBI producers.

MacRae by only one point.

From 1975 to 1988, Brett batted above .300 ten times, had over 100 RBIs four times, and topped 100 runs scored four times. In 1979 he got 85 extra-base hits, and became only the sixth player in history having 20 or more doubles, triples, and home runs in the same season.

The high point of his career was the 1980 season when George batted over .400 most of the year, then dipping the last week of the season to end with .390, just five hits short of .400. It was the highest batting average by any third baseman in more than 70 years and second-highest average overall since Ted Williams. At the same time, George got 118 RBIs in 117 games—the first time anyone had scored more than one RBI per game since 1950. He also hit 24 homers while striking out only 22 times. For these accomplishments, Brett was selected for the AL's MVP award. Ten years later, Brett again won the AL batting title with a .329 average. Few athletes have won batting titles separated by so many years.

Brett improved his fielding and base-running, becoming the most productive player in Royals history. Because of this, the Royals offered Brett the rarest of all things: a lifetime contract. His leadership and batting resulted in a world championship for the Royals in 1985.

Wade Boggs

Wade Boggs has an easy left-handed stroke that sprays line drives to all fields. He also has an outstanding eye for the strike zone, and a well-established routine for keeping himself in perfect shape. Boggs is that rarest of players—a hitter whose statistics are so amazing that he can only be compared with the very greatest of the game. In the post-World War II era of declining batting averages, Boggs' .356 career mark

Wade Boggs is another Red Sox hitting machine, in the tradition of Ted Williams.

puts him fourth behind Ty Cobb, Rogers Hornsby and Joe Jackson.

Boggs reached the majors in 1982, and got his opportunity to play third base for the Red Sox when Carney Lansford injured his ankle. Boggs hit .349 the rest of the season and set an AL rookie record for batting average. The following year he won his first batting title with a .361 average. He topped 200 hits and 100 runs for the first of six years in a row, setting a major league record.

From 1985 until 1990, Boggs never hit below .357. He routinely walks more than 100 times a season, and his on-base percentage for his career is an unmatched .448. In one season (1985), Boggs reached base 340 times. This is a feat only Ruth, Williams and Gehrig had done before him.

Like Cobb, Boggs is superstitious. He runs pre-game windsprints precisely at 7:17 each evening. He draws a Hebrew letter in the batter's box before each at-bat. And his route to and from the playing field is so precise that by late summer his footprints are clearly visible in the grass in front of the Fenway Park dugout.

The great hitters in baseball are a rare breed. Quick, smart and strong, they put together hits in clusters and make this most difficult of all ballgames look easy.

Will there be even greater hitters tomorrow? Only time will tell. Fans of baseball are always hoping that one day a new kid will walk out of the dugout and amaze the world. This kid will defy the laws of physics with smoking drives that will bring back memories of Cobb, Ruth, Williams and the dozens of other great hitters who have made the game of baseball the national pastime.

Glossary

CURVEBALL. A pitch that curves before reaching the plate.

FAIR-FOUL HIT. A pre-1900 rule that a ball was fair even if it rolled foul before reaching first base.

FASTBALL. A pitch thrown as hard as possible into the strike zone.

HOOK SLIDE. The base slide invented by Ty Cobb.

KNUCKLEBALL. A pitch thrown with the knuckles only.

SCREWBALL. A type of curveball.

SPITBALL. An illegal pitch; the pitcher puts grease or spit on the ball to make it harder to hit.

Bibliography

Astor, Gerald. *The Baseball Hall of Fame 50th Anniversary Book.* New York: Prentice-Hall, 1985.

Laird, A.W. *Ranking Baseball's Elite.* McFarland Press, 1990.

Mercurio, John A. *Record Profiles of Baseball's Hall of Famers.* Perennial Press, 1990.

Okrent, Daniel and Steve Wulf. *Baseball Anecdotes.* New York: Oxford University Press, 1989.

Porter, David L. *Biographical Dictionary of American Sports, Baseball.* Greenwood Press, 1987.

Reichler, Joseph, ed. *The Baseball Encyclopedia, 8th ed.* New York: Macmillan, 1990.

Shatzki, Mike ed. *The Ballplayers.* New York: Arbor House, 1990.

Index

Photo Credits

ALLSPORT USA: 6 (Will Hart); 7 (Mike Powell); 8, 30, 41 (Otto Greule, Jr.);
    12, 32 (Jonathan Daniel); 13, 34 (Rick Stewart); 16 (John Swart); 22
    (Allen Dean Steele); 28, 39 (Stephen Dunn); 42 (Don Smith); 44
    (Damian Strohmeyer)
AP Wide World Photos: 20
National Baseball Library, Cooperstown, NY: 14, 18, 19, 24, 26, 36